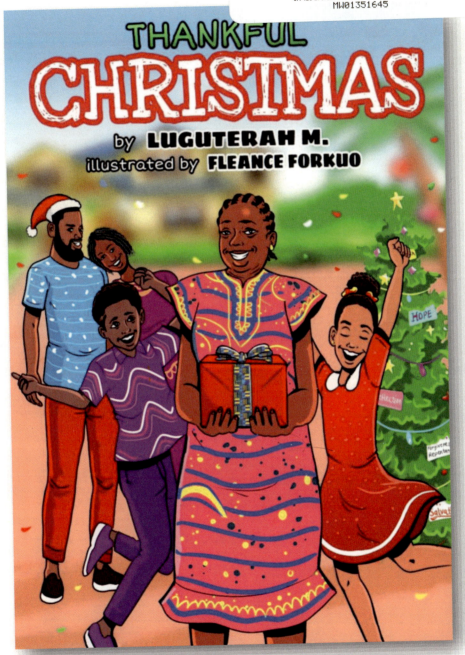

Thankful Christmas is a work of fiction. Names, characters, businesses, places, events, locales, and incidents are either the products of the author's imagination or used in a fictitious manner. Any resemblance to actual persons, living or dead, or actual events is purely coincidental.

Copyright © 2021 by Luguterah. M

All rights reserved including the right to reproduce this book or portions thereof in any form whatsoever. For more information, email mercy.luguterah@gmail.com

Printed in the United States of America

ISBN: 978-1-7374347-2-6 - Paperback version
ISBN: 978-1-7374347-3-3- eBook version

Publisher information: Lugusdesk

I dedicate this book to young children
around the globe.
May you experience peace, hope and love
this season, and all year through.

One early Saturday morning in October, David woke up to a text from his 74 year old mom, Mama Mansa.
It was 7:00am and the text read: *Please call me back as soon as you can. I have some exciting news to share with you.*

Naturally, David was excited but anxious. He wondered what this good news could be. So without hesitation, he called his mom right away.

"Good morning mom, I hope everything is okay with you. I just read your text. What is this great news you have to share?" David asked.

"David! David! David! Remember it's afternoon here in Ghana. You always forget that Ghana is 5 hours ahead of the U.S.," Mama Mansa replied.

"Sorry mom," said David. "My excitement got the best of me. Please tell me the good news."

"Well, there are actually 2 good news. I will tell you one over the phone, but the 2nd, you will have to travel down to Ghana this December to experience it," said Mama Mansa.

"Mom, traveling to Ghana this December will be challenging. It's really short notice, David replied reluctantly."

"I know son, but it is very important to me," Mama Mansa answered endearingly.

"I already made special plans for Christmas here in the U.S. with your grandchildren. They will be disappointed if I change those plans. Can the second news wait until Spring Break in March/April?" David asked.

"No," said Mama Mansa. "That will be too late. Believe me son, you really want to be in Ghana this Christmas. The surprise cannot wait past December."

David knew that his mom was not one to relent in her request, so after 30 minutes of negotiations, he began to entertain the idea of traveling to Ghana with his family in December.

To achieve this, there were lots of steps he needed to take and considerations to be made. So he took a piece of paper and began to write down his to-do list. He called it, "the impossible trip list."

Below is what he wrote:

"THE IMPOSSIBLE TRIP" TO-DO LIST

1. Inform Abena about grandma's request.
2. Request vacation time off from work to travel to Ghana.
3. Get estimates on ticket prices from at least 4 travel sites.
4. Inform children about change of plans.
5. Ensure that everyone's passport is current.
6. Purchase gifts/souvenirs for friends and family in Ghana.

Throughout the day, David muttered, "O mama, mama, mama, she is up to her old tricks again. I wonder what she has to say. O mama, mama, mama."

Just then, it struck him that he didn't ask Mama Mansa about the 1st good news so he called back to speak with her.

By this time, it was already 1:00pm in the U.S. "Mom, you forgot to tell me the good news. What is it?"

"I thought you would never ask," chuckled Mama Mansa. "Remember the community building project I discussed with you about 2 years ago?"

"Mmm, yes I do mama," David replied.

"Well, it's completed." Mama Mansa sang in excitement and continued. "The library, recreation and mentoring center for young children in the community will begin operations this December. Isn't that wonderful?"

"Wow, this is really good news mama. The children will have a safe and quiet place to study, play or be mentored. I'm so glad that our family was able to support this important project. This is a collective dream come true. A well-stocked library in the community is such a legacy for children."

"Yes David, that's why I couldn't wait to share the good news," Mama Mansa replied excitedly.

"I can hear the excitement in your voice mama. I've got to go now Mama, but I will call you again within the week to provide updates about the December trip," said David.

Later that evening when Abena returned home from work, David informed her of Mama's request.

"Hmmm, that's a tough request," Abena responded. "But knowing Mama and given that we haven't seen her in over two years due to COVID-19, I think we should honor her request. I know the children will be disappointed, but they will understand the reason once it's explained to them."

"Let's hope so," David answered with a shoulder shrug.

At dinner, David and Abena took turns explaining to their 7 year old twin children, Isabel (Izzy) and Ajombura about the change of plans.

Ajombura understood the situation and willingly agreed to defer his Christmas celebration, but Izzy was not having it. She began to sob uncontrollably and refused to be consoled. When David attempted to comfort her, she left the table.

Abena followed Izzy to her room, gave her a bear hug and said, "I'm sorry you feel disappointed about the change of plans but it was not intentional. Grandma has important news to share with Dad and we all need to go see her."

"Can't grandma share the news over the phone or even on Zoom? She can still see us via Zoom and it will be the same thing as being there, wouldn't it," asked Izzy.

"That's a fair question Izzy. But meeting in person is not the same as speaking with grandma via zoom. At least grandma does not think it's the same thing," replied Abena.

"Why does grandma get to choose when we travel to Ghana?" Izzy asked through her sob.

"Oh sweetie," Abena wrapped her arms around Izzy. "I understand. The truth is, sometimes when we make good plans, unexpected things happen that change those plans. It doesn't mean our plan was not good or important, it just means that we would have to delay it a little while in order to fulfill a more urgent request."

"I still don't get it, mom."

"My dear, I know you love grandma and besides, you have never been to Ghana, so this could be an exciting opportunity for you and your brother. I promise you that dad and I will make it up to you and your brother when we return from the trip. I triple promise," said Abena.

At this time, Izzy had stopped sobbing and was listening attentively to her mom. "You triple promise?" She asked.

"Yes princess, I triple promise. I will make it up to you," replied Abena, kissing her daughter's forehead before Izzy wrapped her arms around her mother's neck.

"It's okay mom," Izzy replied. "I accept your triple promise. But what did Ajombura say about the change in plans?"

Abena smiled and rubbed her nose against Izzy's. "Your brother is busy enjoying seconds of his dinner. But, he was okay with the change as long as we made it up to you both."

"Mom, can I ask you a question?"

"Mmm."

"How come Ajombura and I are very different?"

Abena gave a hearty laugh. "Sweetheart, that's a question that I am still seeking answers for."

Izzy managed a smile to that response and agreed to the trip.

"Thank you Izzy," said Abena.

"What for," Izzy asked her mother with a puzzling look on her face.

"For letting me know how you felt about the change in plans. I assure you that your dad and I will always give a listening ear to your thoughts and perceptions, even if we won't always agree with them. This home will always be a safe space and place for you and your brother."

"I already know that mom," replied Izzy, chuckling as she hugged her mother again.

Over the next couple of months, Ajombura worked on his *Ghana Christmas plans* judiciously.

December 15th came around and it was time to catch a flight from IAD Dulles Airport to Kotoka International Airport in Accra, Ghana.

After an 11 hour long flight, the family was finally in Ghana.

On the other side of the arrival hall was Mama Mansa smiling and waving with such enthusiasm that she could not be missed.

"Akwaaba (welcome) my babies," Mama Mansa spread her arms joyfully to embrace Ajombura and Izzy. "Akwaaba David and Abena. Thank you for coming. I really appreciate the sacrifice."

"That's okay, grandma. We are happy to be here," replied Abena and David.

"Dad says you have some good news to share with us all and we can't wait to hear it," Ajombura quipped as grandma led everyone through the airport to the car waiting outside. She promised to share the news soon enough.

On the 45 minute drive home from the Airport, Izzy and Ajombura starred in amazement at the housing architecture they were engulfed in.

"Wow, this is amazing. Such beautiful buildings just like the U.S.!" Izzy exclaimed.

"No! Its better than the U.S.," quipped Ajombura. "We have to take pictures to show our friends in the U.S."

Grandma smiled and said, "You haven't seen anything yet. There are so many beautiful places to visit."

Early the next morning, before 6am, Izzy and Ajombura heard what sounded like an animal in distress. Grandma explained that it was just a cock crowing, and that they should expect to hear that sound everyday around the same time. "Like a natural alarm clock," asked Izzy.

Grandma chuckled. "Yes, that's an excellent description."

"This is super incredible," replied Izzy.

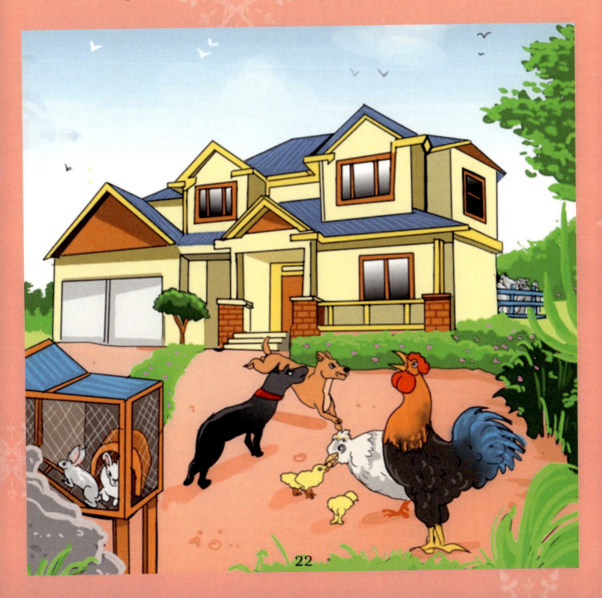

At breakfast time, the doorbell rang and everyone wondered who this early guest could be.

Kwame, the home aide, answered the door, and in walked Ellen (David's older sister) with her husband and 2 children. "Surprise! Surprise!" Yelled Ellen.

Everyone, including Izzy and Ajombura screamed in excitement.

"What are you doing here? You are supposed to be in Canada?" exclaimed Abena.

"We arrived in Ghana two days ago. As to what we're doing here, you will have to ask grandma. She said she has some great news to share," Ellen replied with a smile.

"Grandma, did you know about all this? What is going on," Abena asked a laughing mama Mansa.

"Grandma, how many more surprises should we expect," asked Ajombura.

"No more surprises children. I promise this is it," Mama Mansa replied. "But I assure you that this is going to be a great Christmas. By the way David, your younger brother Oscar is also in town. He arrived from Australia a week ago. You will all get to see him tomorrow," she concluded.

"Can you tell us the good news now," asked Izzy and Ajombura.

"Not yet my love, I will share the good news with everyone on Christmas day," their grandmother replied.

With a few days to Christmas, grandma was busy with the preparations of the special Christmas meal.

Izzy and Ajombura spent the next few days overcoming their jet lag and playing with the neighborhood kids. They learnt to play traditional Ghanaian games like *oware*, *ampe* and *pilolo*. Each day was like an adventure because they learnt something new and got to spend ample time outdoors.

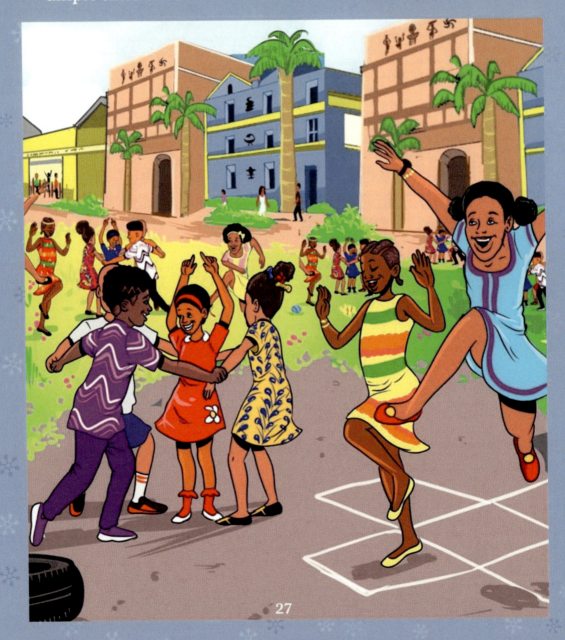

Izzy and Ajombura were surprised to see that it was very common for chickens, goats, and sheep to roam the streets or share the same common space with humans.

And what about houses made with red sand? They had never seen those either.

Even amazing was the fact that they had so much fun within a relatively short time playing outdoors than they ever did indoors with their electronic devices.

Finally, Christmas Eve came around.

"Now I can't wait for the good news grandma, you only have a few more hours to go so you must tell us when the time comes," Izzy told her grandmother.

"Don't worry my little loves, I sure will share the news. But first things first. In the morning, when we wake up, everyone is going to chip in to help prepare our Christmas meal," Mama Mansa reminded the children.

"Sounds like a good plan," yelled Ajombura. "I can't wait to eat," as he proceeded to the bedroom. "Hang on, how about Christmas presents? It's Christmas eve and I don't see any Christmas trees or presents. No stockings either."

"That's true," Angie (Ellen's daughter) replied. "I hope Santa makes it to grandma's house before tomorrow morning."

Koko (Ellen's son) tapped on his lips a few times, looking around Mama Mansa's living room. "I don't see a chimney in this house or any house in this neighborhood for that matter. How will Santa enter the house?"

Grandma laughed so loudly that her belly jellied. "Don't worry children, something greater than Santa is going to happen."

On Christmas morning, the aroma of various delicacies filled the air. Mama Mansa and the parents were busy in the kitchen. It took countless hours to prepare the Christmas meal.

By noontime, it was all done and folks were ready to eat.

"Phew! Finally," exclaimed Izzy. "Why did the food take so long to prepare?"

At grandma's request, a specially crafted long wooden dining table was carefully placed in the open courtyard of grandma's house, and the gates were left wide open. This way, neighbors and anyone passing by could stop in at anytime during the day to enjoy a free Christmas meal.

"Ahhh, now I know why we prepared so much food," said Ajombura.

Overlooking the dining table were 4 tall coconut trees with ripened coconuts in need of rescuing. When the table was all set, it was a sight to behold.

Call it the international feasting table; there was Jollof Rice, Fried Chicken, Hot and Spicy Chili Sauce (Shito), Sourdough Dumpling (Kenkey) with Fried Fish, Rice and Bean combination (Waakye), Granulated Cassava Flour (Gari) with Beans and Plantain, cooked slightly-fermented mixture of Corn-dough and Cassava dough (Banku) with Okra Soup, Fresh Ginger Juice and Hibiscus drink (Sobolo).

When the family was seated, grandma asked David to say grace.

"Yes, mama, you got it. I'm always ready to say grace." David asked everyone to bow their head as he said these few words: "Thank you God for food, life, family and good health. Bless the food we are about to eat, and keep us safe from harms way, in Jesus name we pray, Amen."

Throughout the day, neighbors stopped in to eat and exchange pleasantries. Some even had the option to take portions of food to their family members.

Izzy and Ajombura had so much fun playing in the courtyard sand and making new friends that they forgot about Santa's visit. Not once did they ask for presents.

Abena and David held each other in warm embrace as they watched their children play.

"I've never seen our children this happy in all the 7 years of their life," Abena said. "They are playing without a care in the world. I think grandma did us a favor by asking us to visit."

David chuckled. "I completely agree with you. She certainly did us a great favor. Do you think this is the good news she wanted to share with us?"

"I doubt this is the good news. I think she really has some important message to share with the family. In the meantime, I think it is important to encourage our children to spend more time outdoors when we return to the U.S. I can already see the many benefits of playing outdoors," responded Abena.

At evening time, grandma gathered her children and grandkids over a cup of hot Milo and begun to speak.

"I know you are wondering what this other good news I have is all about. Now it's time to tell you."
Everyone gathered around grandma with excitement and paid full attention to her as she continued speaking.

"Over the past 2 years, I have realized more than ever the importance of family and good relationships. I appreciate the great house and cars you children have provided for me, but I understand better now the essence of family."

Ellen, David, Abena, Ellen's husband and the children all nodded in agreement to Mama Mansa while she continued to speak.

"I lost a few friends to the pandemic. They had so many plans and lots of ideas to accomplish but they run out of time. Before I or anyone runs out of time, I wanted to let you know this rare truth:

If you wake up each day and are surrounded by family and or loved ones, do know that you are truly blessed. You have everything you need!"

"I'm not saying you shouldn't work hard or make plans, but I don't want you to miss out on the important things in life such as family and fellowship. I see how you work so hard abroad and hardly have time to rest. You are always on the go when I call. I knew that if I asked you to come on a regular visit, you wouldn't have come right away, but if I mentioned about the good news, you would be compelled to come. Indeed, this is good news, that I have everything I already need, and so do you."

Mama Mansa took a sip of her hot milo drink and smiled at her family. "No better time to remind you of this important fact than Christmas. Izzy and Ajombura, I heard you ask about Santa and presents. Don't worry, grandma has lots of presents for you and yes, Santa visits Ghana too."

All the children clapped in excitement. Izzy even jumped a few times at the mention of Christmas presents.

Mama Mansa stretched her arms and Izzy sat on her lap. "But my greatest gift this year is that I get to see you in-person for the first time in 7 years."

"Oh grandma, we're so glad to see you too," Ajombura added. He soon joined Izzy on Mama Mansa's lap.

"Christmas is about love, hope, reflection, appreciation, forgiveness, giving, peace, repentance, salvation, and a new beginning."

Mama Mansa took a deep breath and continued. "I hope that you experience all of this for yourself. Most importantly, I hope that you extend the same to others when you return home."

"Awwww, grandma, I'm so happy mom and dad agreed to bring us to Ghana. I cried when mom said we would have to change our Christmas plans to come see you. Hugging you is so much better than speaking with you on a tablet. We will never forget this feeling. We love you grandma, we love you so much. We will surely visit you again very soon," said Izzy.

"Yes, we do," affirmed Ajombura.

On the flight back to the US, Izzy rolled over to Abena and said, "Mom, I know you triple promised to make it up to me, but you don't really have to. I had so much fun. I'm truly thankful I got to share this moment with grandma and the neighborhood children."

"A promise is a promise Izzy," Abena replied. "I will still make it up to you but I'm glad you had fun."

Personalized "Thankful Christmas" Poem

Luguterah, M. is a Ghanaian-American Montessori educator and writer who has devoted sixteen years of her professional career working with children ages 9 and below. Luguterah possesses a PhD in Behavioral Sciences, a Master's degree in Social Work and a Second Masters in Development Studies. It's been her life-long passion to impact young lives through story-telling. An adjunct faculty member at University of Maryland Global Campus (UMGC) since 2013, and a blogger at Lugusdesk.com, her interests include community service, singing and fitness.

Illustrator Biography

Fleance Forkuo is a Ghanaian based artist. A graduate of Kumasi Anglican, Fleance discovered his passion for drawing at a young age. With the unflinching support of his parents and family members, he nurtured his talent and has gone on to create amazing artwork and illustrations for many. His mission is to use his gift as a tool to brighten this world.

Acknowledgements

All that I have or hope to become, I owe it all to God Almighty, the Savior and Keeper of my soul. Thank you Lord for the journey of my life. I acknowledge you now and always. I'm forever grateful for your daily mercies and guidance. I live because you live.

To my dear mom, Alice Fati Takara Mahama, thank you for being you. I'm grateful for all the sacrifices you have made and continue to make for me. I appreciate you so much.

To my dad, I say much respect to you. You've always believed in me.

To the many strangers who showed me kindness when I least expected it, I acknowledge you, I appreciate you.

To family, friends and my Holy Child School squad, your continued support is what keeps me going. Thank you for all you do for me.

To B11, you will always hold a special place in my heart.

To my BEST FRIEND, I say thank you. You make my life beautiful each day. What an awesome human being you are. I am so blessed to have you in my life. I appreciate you.

To Olatunde @thereallavenderMe, thank you for elevating my work and bringing it to life. I owe you one.

May all who read this story be inspired to recognize the important blessings that surround them each day.

Made in the USA
Middletown, DE
12 December 2021